G.O.D.

by

B. L. Peterson

<u>Dedicated to:</u>
<u>The Governing Operating Denizens</u>
<u>of the World.</u>
<u>G.O.D.'s</u>

<u>G.O.D.</u>

**The Governing Operating Denizens are a Group of trained
Denizens who perform and create Physical, Psychic, PSI, and
Transcendental Activities and Exercises for the betterment of all
Denizens, Paragons, and all
Spiritual Beings {SP's} in existence.**

**What makes them super special is that they
Are dedicated to helping all of mankind with no regard to race,
Nationality, Sex gender, or any other modifications of the
HUMAN BEING {H. S.}.**

**No SPIRITUAL BEING {SP} is obligated to help anyone else
besides himself. This is because man can only save himself by
himself and one's job is to be done as one's job and not another
job of someone else.**

**You can only take people to the Universal Ball, you can't make
them dance.**

We thank all G. O. D.'s for making this a better world for all.

Table of Contents

Chapter Six:
Outro
The Vi-Guru
Pg. 89

<u>INTRO</u>

G.O.D.

Governing Operating Denizens

Man has been programmed for ages to think he is a 'body with a
soul' that can be thrown into heaven or hell when he dies.
The TRUTH is man is a 'SOUL with a mind, body, and
environment' in which he is trying to survive as a temporary
MATTER-ENERGY unit in a SPACE-TIME continuum.
This is the same as saying:
Man is an ETERNAL BEING with an INFINITE MIND in a FINITE
BODY/Environment.
You are a SPIRIT.
You are your own SOUL.
You are not moral.
You can be happy and free.

This is probably one of the hardest chapters to write, for things
are rarely at the pace and the time and the place and space and
energy-flow that I want to write in.
Everything has got to be some sort of effort, some sort of
struggle, or fighting within when
it should be effortless by now,
I mean SPIRIT is really effortless-
It is a 'cause' with, and without effect.
And yet,
It is not
First Cause.
But the last curse,
meaning you are being what
You don't want to be.
Doing what you don't want to do,

Though you are doing what you think you like.
And you know you will get a great reward someday
For all your efforts and sacrifices.

"There will be Pie in the sky,
When you die,
Is a lie."

Letting God change Your Mind.
Change Your Heart.
Change Your World.
But God does not change.
Only He changes everything.

Yet,
What you think about God,
How you see God,
How you know God,

How do you see the real God from the false gods?

Is there a real God?
Or did we create Him in our OWN Image?
Or did He create us in His OWN Image?
And what is The IMAGE of God?

Are we still living in fear of
Death and the Unknown?

Did we become gods,
or invisible ears?

Is God done,
or yet to come?

The
Being-Non-being Continuum,
Continues…

This is how one knows the real God.
The real, living God, not the dead energy created one.

GOD IS A PERFECT STATIC

For none other entity can
fit that Position which
Is not a Position at all,
but for our edification:
We call it
The Seat of God.
The Highest State of Super Consciousness.
The Perfect Static of God.
The perfect static of the Self.

As long as you have life,
part of you 'acts' as a
kinetic.
And part of you is like a 'Standing Wave.
This is the same static that God is part of that you are a part of.

His Perfect Static is your 'perfect peace, love, and happiness in
the PSI {spiritual}, Psychic, and Physical Worlds.

To this point and reason,
no living entity {man or woman}
can be fully God in the flesh,
But God can be fully 'YOU' in
your flesh.

It is like One fits into the other perfectly,
and when you try and reverse the roles,
It just does not work-
The limited can contain only so much of the

Limitless-
Whereas,
The Limitless can contain
all of the limited and even
surpass it in its limitations.

If you know God,
It is because God revealed
Himself to you.

Of this you can be certain.
For He {and we use the masculine term}
is
THE ETERNAL SOURCE and LIFEFORCE
of which all people, places and particles
flow and ebb.
You came from God. You live in God's Mind. You go back to God
when you die.

Nothing exist outside of God,
not even 'nothing'.

Welcome to
The Plane of Creative Realities.
The Psychic Plane.

Here You are
Sovereign King of this world,
Your own psychic world.
And God let's you be god
Of your world, with

All of His Power at your disposal.

TRUTH here is what God feels.
YOU FEEL.
And God always feels good.
Super-Good.
The highest vibration of the universe.

And He is that Super-good feeling in you.

Bring your body and mind into
Alignment with God's Divine Reality:
For He is
The Source of All TRUTHS and LIES.

And He is The Ultimate Reality in and behind it all.
And Creator of illusions and delusions
at your own will.

It is not a lack of God's Power that
makes man unhappy,

But the limited use
that comes with
bad religion,
and other things
that enslaves the mind.

And man has little or no power at all.

But Power is for the responsible
And therefore is hidden from the Masses.

For the responsible who are
responsible for their actions,
Have no problem with Power.
It is only a matter of
Self-discipline.

Do your PSI-40 exercises.

I am more than grateful to
give you Space and Time
to do this.

For you take super good care
of My Agents.
And they take better care of You.
We pay them well.
And do not tell.
That we take 'souls'
Right out of hell.

You gave more than
You ever received.
You blessed more
Then eyes have seen.

You open our eyes to the
Abundance of
being a
Spiritual Being {SP}.

Let us drop any false pride,
any 'guilt' that hides,

'old doubts', and 'loving {binding} ties'.

For on the whirlwind
Still we ride---
How we lied.
How we cried.
How we died.

Waiting for our take
At a higher pay rate.
It never came,
The Problems the same.

For it is not money or weed or speed or Thee that
we need.
But only to Work, Play, Rest, and Sleep in
Peace.

We abandon the Edgar Allen Poe complex.
The Lewis Carroll complex.
Even Stephen King has got to go…
The Starving {Crazy} Artist has got to go!

Now maybe my style will really show.
As my very own!

"For 'Truth' is you,
my friend.
And God is your
Eternal Friend,
who has no beginning

And no end.”

The
Magnetic-electrical field
Bio-electrical field
Psi-chi field
All make up your Light Body.

THE GIVER WITHIN.
THE GIVER WITHOUT.
THE TAKER WITHIN.
THE TAKER WITHOUT.
IS THIS WHAT LIFE
IS REALLY ALL ABOUT?

“With or without God
Obey the Laws of the Land,
My friend,
And keep ‘Clean Hands’.”

For if you are not living in your own reality,
You are living in someone else’s.

If this makes you happy,
I am happy for you-

It matter not to Me if
you be Master or slave-

For I too am Servant of
The Most High.

For there is none above It
or below It.
Outside of It.
Beyond it or around It.

The Living God…
Not the dead Ones!

This is
Transcendental Knowledge.

PSI-40 is one of the most advanced Physical, Psychic, Spiritual,
and Transcendental Technology available to man today. It is
newer than it is old.
It is complete, but it is not finished.

For one who Master's PSI-40 in months, years, decades?
He will be prepared to research and write other PSI
EMPOWERMENT BOOKS, using
PSI-40 as a basis.

PSI-40 is the first of it's kind and stands as a Basis for all
Transcendental books.

If some pseudo Transcendental book comes out and does not
agree with us,
at least in part, I would be careful of its information.

It it does not work for you, even if I said it, or you read it,
Disregard it.

SPIRIT gives life and life abundant.
Not Death or Dying!
There is no such thing as a DEAD SPIRIT or DEAD SOUL!

And since SPIRIT is Eternal, there is no shortage of life except
in the limited mind that 'believes' there is a lack of Spirit or Life.
Belief is a killer.
Either you KNOW or don't KNOW.

You UNDERSTAND or you don't UNDERSTAND.
YOU USE or YOU DON'T USE.

Quit fooling {lying to} yourself.
Don't live a lie.
Know yourself, and you know God.
It matters not if you are gay, straight, bi, or trans-sexual.
Your Spiritual or Divine Life has nothing to do
with your sexual gender.
Just like It does not care if you are rich or poor.
A rich man can be just as Divine as a poor man.
So can a Black man be just as Divine, if not more,
than any white or brown man.
Skin color has nothing to do with your Spiritual Life,
except it is a variation in human beings.
Being a Spiritual Being, the primal nature of what
You truly are, has to do with knowing the
Transcendental Knowledge that
You are not your body and mind.
Even God has a sex life, and can
have Lovers and Friends
A boyfriend or girlfriend,
A wife or a husband,

**Or live a singular Life of no sex for the sake of a
Higher Purpose.**

<u>PSI -40</u>
<u>Part One</u>

Now is the place and time to use
Your PSI and Psychic Powers.
This is what PSI-40 is all about.

In the past,
When I use to share my knowledge of
the Power within you,
Even some of my best friends would learn what I said,
Then use the Power against me to see if it worked or not?
I don't know.
Be careful who you give 'power' {knowledge} too.
But after several times of this happening
To me, I learned to keep my mouth shut.
In other words,
Silence is golden.

If you follow these Guidelines none of your experiences will
backfire on you.
And if they do…Spirit will restore you to where you 'went wrong'
and not
take you backwards.
For the Present will always be fresh and new to you.
And you will be too.

WATCH your posture.
Negative people and gravity tends to pull you down.
Let the Gravity of the Sun pull you up, keep your back strong and
straight and your head high.

Keep your aura clean and pure, and it will automatically stay
positive, and help you stay positive.
Cry in the night if you have too.
Face your fears and demons {negative thoughts and emotions}.
Face your fears is facing your inner conflicts.
Admit that they are there.
Feel them and let them go.
Restore your Positive Attitude by meditating
on one of your Secret words or a mantra.
You can pray to God, but most people pray
to a negative or pseudo-god and get little or
No results or solutions to their problems.

Face your inner conflicts without judgement
or condemning yourself.
This is the best way to handle a problem.

Remember, this too, shall pass.

And you have ¾ Positive Power to ¼ Negative Resistance to work
and play with.
Be not afraid of psychic disturbance or conflicts.
Again face your fears and they will melt away
into nothingness, without any conscious conflict.

Spirit is ¾ Positive Energy to the ¼ Negative Energy of the
world.

You can't lose.

Spirit will give you the courage to do the possible as well as the
impossible.

The reason of this Introduction is to let you know as a Psychic,
you will encounter psychic and physical experiences, good and
bad.
Psychic disturbances decrease as you grow
stronger spiritually.
And you will encounter strange new lands, new ideas,
and physical and psychic adventures all because your
CONSCIOUSNESS is EXPANDING like the physical Universal.

YOU ARE IN MOTION.

You may be the first Pioneer in a field never dealt with
psychically before and you may help to bring its true meaning to
the world.

Since this world is ¼ negative, people are negative by choice and
force, other people's 'limited minds', and unknown reasons.

There are beings in the world, such as us, but not as
knowledgeable, who can control others from a distance and 'act'
upon them without even being in the same room.

Be not display as you come to know your Self,
the parts of you, you like and don't like.

You will know your 'own thoughts' and 'feelings' from those
of another.
You will be your own unique man or woman.

For you are a unique Spiritual Being {SP} already.

With ¼ of this world under the illusion of slack and lack
you don't have to believe it or agree with this negative world.

Remember, the Greatest Light is always IN YOU.

There is no God 'outside' of you,
that is not 'inside' of you.

If all the physical sun and moon and stars were shining in your
psyche-
It still would not be as bright as your LIGHT BODY.

Think of the glories and bliss in the Spiritual Universe

that needs no outside Light to be Illuminate and illuminating.

The Beings here are Self-shining, and Self-existence, Self-loving,
and Self-caring, and Self-sufficient like God.

Who loves all His Devotees more.

God does not play favorites like men and women do, but He
helps His devotees and destroys the 'demon or slave-mind.'

Now you have the Ksatriyas at your assistance.
They operate in every race like 'angels' and 'angles'.

They help everyone and they are only licensed
by The Bhuta Bhavana and the Bhutesas.
They aid humans, gods, and demi-gods in all aspects.
They do not kill or harm anyone for all their actions are
only PSI and psychic in a positive way.

The Ksatriyas are not as positive as the higher order of Beings in
the Higher Spiritual worlds,
Because they fall down at times, but they always find a way to
pick themselves up and resume what they were doing or start
something new.

And Spirit is always right there, where he or she went 'wrong' to
lead them again, into the right way.

Ksatriyas are Masters of Evolution, Involution, and Devolution.

If you can assist them in any way and it is in your power, do so,
for a miracle might happen in your sphere of Life {Living}.

Good results always follow the assisting of any Kshatriyas.

Psychic Entities are very rewarding.

But God rewards all.

Ksatriyas are Psychic Warriors and make perfect Spirit Guides
to Psychic Entities {PE}.

But today people's souls are
sick, split, vexed, cursed, and ill.

And guess what?
It is all a lie!
It is all an illusion and especially
the delusions of others.

They are the illusion taken for Gospel Truth!

Held in place by 'fear' called 'faith'.

That is why the person suffers. That is why the person is in pain and knows not why.

He KNOWS that something is wrong, but has no idea of what is causing it, or how to get rid of it.

Even his good actions can bring him more pain and misery than happiness.

He pours his heart out to a girl and it is tramped under.
He tries to be good and successful; gets so far and falls on his face.
And in his mind, constantly fighting the words:

"You are the worst person." "You cannot succeed, so quit!"
"You are no good and your work is no good." "You don't have the right mind or skills." "Stop! It will happen tomorrow!" "God will do it for you." "You are useless." "You are worthless."
"You have no value or talents."

These negative statements are common language in the world today. They get in your mind and work havoc!
We call them {N.E.T.} Negative Electronic Traps!
They are the language of the SLAVE mind, a stimulus/response archaic system.

Psi-40 will help you eliminate this negative chatter in your head, and help free up the 1/4 of your mind which is Negative to a totally Pure, Free, Positive, Powerful, and Pristine Super Mind and Consciousness.

You are dealing with the most powerful POWER in the universe and in the world and in existence. And it is GOOD.

Because it is LIFE and LIFE ETERNAL.

You can live in heaven now, without having to die, or be insane, while you are still alive in your physical body or out of your physical body.

God made a way for us to survive in the universe but it is only found in Him for He is the Ultimate Reality where all things exist and can be true.

God exists in all His various forces and forms.
And you, as you are, are one of them.

Knowing that you are the supreme part of this Power should give you confidence that you can achieve all your goals.

But we all can achieve our goals with proper planning and self-control.

God gives to everyone exactly what they want, but most people want bad things and get them and blame the devil or Satan for getting them and making their life miserable.

"BE CAREFUL WHAT YOU ASK FOR?"
NO!
"BE CAREFUL WHAT YOU DON'T ASK FOR."

YOU POSSESS ALL AND YOU POSSESS GOD, AND GOD POSSESSES YOU!

You are in God and God is in you!
This is the complete whole-the serpent bites his tail. The perfect
balance of Yin and Yang!

You are complete in Spirit and Power.
You have all the Power you need,
To be happy and free and to live a happy and free life here and
now and not in some distant future that might never come.

You can grow mentally and spiritually
and help yourself and others.
or
do nothing at all, and rest in comfort as a Spiritual Being {SP}.
And the fun part is that you can do it in any way you like.

We are all going in the same direction,
Just on different Paths.
We all are Spiritual Beings {SP} having a human experience on
earth.
You only got so much 'earth time' use it wisely!

But be responsible to the responsible.
Be responsible for yourself.
Keep your word and don't make promises you can't keep.
The best way to keep your word,
is not to give it.

Don't blame God if you jump off a bridge and don't fly like a bird.

There are His Natural Law, you know as
The Laws of Mother Nature.
They will break you, before you will break them.

God gave you a good, perfect functioning brain.
It is not His fault if you do not use it.

If it is damage or faulty,
Use it to the best of your ability.

Trust in God and He or She will help you,
Depending on how you look at It.
Trust in God and God will trust in you.
Have faith in yourself and God will have faith in you!

The Lifeforce of all force and forms
is One in two parts that makes three.

THE FATHER/MOTHER/SPIRIT{BEING}
creates the Living Beings that we are.

Male and Female, It created us,
Black and White, Tall and Short.

In all varieties It created a beautiful person and a beautiful earth
we must all also take care of.

If we blow it up,
Where will we go?
Where will we live?

PSI-40
Part two

Recently,
I did extensive work on my karma.

Karma is simply the natural law of
cause and effect.

For every cause,
There is an equal or opposite effect.
Bad or Negative karma is
karma built up that
effect you in a negative
or a depressing way.

It is normally subconscious and
Therefore goes undetected
For years and years.

By erasing or transforming
Negative karma into
Positive karma,
you will find that
you are less fearful
and have a keener sense of your
surroundings, body and mind as being more positive than
negative.

Beware now of the negativity of other people.

Embrace it! Love it and Hear it.
But don't 'buy' into it.

The Eternal Fire within you will burn up anything positive or
negative that is not serving your best interest.

This is why there is no negativity in
THE MASTERMIND
of the Universe.

As your Positive karma is release
you become more of a
Spiritual Being {SP: Spiritual Person}.

As a Spiritual Being {SP} you are able to be more objective in
your viewpoint.

And you are in a 'spiritual position' that is the best place to be for
the proper control and creation of your happy life and destiny.

When you 'merge' into God,
You do not lose your
Individuality of who you are,
In fact,
You become more of
who You truly are.

What is wonderful about
God is that God contains
All your wants and desires,
And will give it to you

As you give them to Him.

And
All you want and desire are manifested

In all His various forces and forms.

It is actually God's Energies
that you enjoy in the
Physical and Psychic worlds.

It becomes what you Will of it.

It is what you will, and what you will
IT IS.

Many books are written on how to
use this neutral force in nature.

This Psychic and Psi Force of the mind.

For it is not for or against you or anyone,
no more than electricity is.
Just as electricity can give us needed light in the dark, it also can
electrocute
you and you are dead.

SPIRIT is an ETERNAL, IMPERSONAL ENERGY we can make
PERSONAL POWER.

It is there for you to use as a
Spiritual Being {SP}.

This same Force is also in your mind
and brain as PSYCHIC ENERGY.

Psychic Energy is what is behind and
activates all your Physical Energy.

And Psychic Energy is controlled
and used by PSI Energy, or Spiritual Energy of old.

It matters not if this Energy is
Holy or not,
Positive or not,
'Believed-in' or not,
IT IS.

And It is at your beckoning call.

What I discovered in the science of MetaPsychics is that
PSI Energy is available to all
and is the Superior Energy
of all the inferior energies
such as the ego, intellect, mind, emotions, thoughts, thinking,
doing, being, having, sensing,
Space, Time, Energy, Matter,
Fire, Air,Water, Earth, Ether, and all 'limited minds and egos'.

The Superior Energy is One.

It does not change but changes everything.

The Inferior Energies are multiple and varied.

Matter of fact,
It, SPIRIT or ETERNAL ENERGY created the stars and the
planets,
the emotions and egos,
And It is the Psychic Power
behind all Minds and Bodies.

This Energy is so Powerful, that one should be 'grounded' before
he attempts to 'use' it.

ANd God lets you 'use' this Energy freely with no charge.

Using this Energy is what God intended.

He did not abandon you here on earth!

He is always giving you ample supply of
all you need and want according
to what you think and feel.

And the Reservoir of this Power is
Unlimitless.

It goes on forever and can
never-ever be destroyed in totality.
And it is with you as well as without you.

Because the Nature of this Power is greater than your physical
body and 'limited slave-mind', it is good and very highly
suggested that one stay 'grounded' when using this Power or
Energy directly.

When one is Grounded,

{His feet firmly on the ground},
He is drawing energies 'up' from the earth.

It enters his feet and goes up his legs, thighs,
gentiles, groin, stomach, solar plexus,
chest, fingers, arms, shoulders,
neck, face, head and exists
out the top of the head and
envelopes the physical body
in what is called your AURA.

You, as a Spiritual Being {SP}
actually radiate Energy outward
like little golden beams of light.

This is actually an Electromagnetic field around your body, just
like the earth has its own Electromagnetic field around it.

This is also called your Light-body, for you are in control of it
and can move it faster than the speed of light.

How fast is the speed of thought?

Of old, this was referred to as your Astral body or Light Body.

It is very real, except you cannot see it with your physical eyes.

It is invisible like your 'soul' which is one of the major reasons
Scientists overlooked the 'soul' of man for so long, and still does.
Religion became the 'study of the soul' for man who did not have
the mental technology he has today. He said the 'soul' was
separated from God and made a religion so you can pay them to

connect you to God again.
That is why this book is so important to you for it tells you the truth.

You are Spiritual Being {SP} having a human experience, NOT a human body with a soul as religion would have you believe.

SPIRIT or ETERNAL ENERGY extends from the Source of your psyche outside the perimeters of your physical body.

And you can even change the color {mood} and personality {atmosphere} of it at will.

In MetaPsychics, we combine
all these words and call your
ego, emotions, thoughts and actions,
your soul or A PARAGON or DENIZEN.

A PARAGON/DENIZEN is the METAPSYCHICS term for the 'soul' or 'jiva' of the body.

Your SOUL is your individualized
Light Body.

Your SOUL is what animates your LIFE.

Your SOUL is the CONSCIOUSNESS of the body and mind and environment.

It is not confined or 'limited' to the physical body
or the slave {limited} mind or even the physical universe.

The Paragon and Denizen are the same thing, Spiritual Beings {SP}, but with different purposes and Paths to travel.

The Denizen travels the Path of Light, as in the way of the Sun, from which the word 'son of God' got its origin.

'Sons of God' referred to mankind, when he was still in his Light-body and had not taken on the more gross earthly, physical form.

It is nothing more than the 'Christian version' of your aura or Light Body called CHRIST, not Jesus!

And your Light Body is your Soul,
And your Soul, or Atman, is you
as a Paragon or Denizen.

The Paragon takes The Path of Day {Light}, for he plans to reincarnate in another physical body instantly, or at some later date.

This is the Mystic Way and more personal than impersonal.

The Denizen takes the Path of Night {Darkness}. {This is not evil, but only another way to the same place.}
This is more the Magical Way and is also private as well as personal.
The Denizen DOES NOT reincarnate, he is on his finally mission on earth and he vows not to return again, though he has that option even if it is billions of trillions of years in the future, or the next day.

A Paragon desires to 'reincarnate' one day {or night}, in another body, most likely of the same race he is in now, or another race and/or nationality.

Spirit is not bound by the limited mind.
SPIRIT is naturally free, not supernatual.

The Limitless cannot be bound by the limited.

This is how you KNOW you found the real
GOD of all,
Creator, Supplier, Transformer, Transcendental.

The same God who is
The Source of all forces and forms
seen and unseen.
The LIVING GOD of the universe not the DEAD GOD of the book!

In It is all things.

Yet, It surpasses all things-
Nothing is outside of It,
Not even 'nothing'.

So not only can you
KNOW
GOD,
You also can also
UNDERSTAND,
GOD,
And
USE

GOD
or
His ENERGIES to
make your life the way
GOD IS...
Perfect,
Pure,
Primal,
Pristine,
Positive,
and
Permanent
ENERGY
and
CONSCIOUSNESS!

There is no hate in the
REAL GOD,
for hate, like jealousy,
and envy,
are of man,
NOT GOD.

**God is an impersonal FORCE till you make Him PERSONAL.
You make God personal by realizing He or It is your Higher
Power, your Higher Self within you, NOT without you as bad
religions would have you believe.**

God has no reason to kill mankind,
when mankind has found so many ways to kill himself.

God is One
In two parts:

The Supersoul of all,
and the
individual soul of all.

You could say that God, your soul {true ego},
and mind {Communicating system} are
Non-dimensional.

While your physical body, the physical world and Universe are
Dimensional.

KNOW THIS AND YOU KNOW THE TRUE, LIVING, GOD which
is the REAL YOU.
Your real EGO {Consciousness}.

THIS GOD IS THE SAME TO EVERYONE.

For He IS the same ENERGY that is in everyone.

God is always the Greater part
of The Whole, and the smallest
part of The Whole and you are
the micro soul of God's Macro Soul
Of the Universe.

Mathematically speaking we have a firm
foundation for the existence of God.
This is CERTAINTY.
We know that we know.

THE FORMULA OF THE TRUE GOD OF ALL IS:

R>0 is the physical Universe.

R=0 is the Infinite Mind.

R=>0 is the soul and Supersoul {God}.

**This formula is a mathematical proof of
the existence of God.**

Before The Big Bang, God was.

**If you think one man or group of men can put the entire scope of
God in one book or a trillion books you are sadly mistaken.**

**We KNOW God exist,
And you should know it to by now too.**

**You can only PROVE God by
USING God.**

When you are still God is STILL WORKING.

When you are moving, God is STILL WORKING.

God is LIFE, not death.

**Death is a dimensional transition of a
Energy composite.**

**The physical body may die and decay,
But the soul lives on,
being made of finer energy
that cannot be created or destroyed.**

God is what survives life and death.

So if there is life and death, and
God represents life and and death, being
the pair of opposites,
there must be a
Transcendental Life of no death-
This would be THE ETERNAL.

And here is the secret
not even Jesus told you...

There is life limited {closed minded}.
There is life Infinite, {abundant and open minded}.
And,
There is Life Eternal {God Conscious} or

TRANSCENDENTAL CONSCIOUSNESS.

For there is death.
Death of the body, even of the psychic, but
NEVER-EVER of the soul.

And there can be Death of the Spirit,
Though the Spirit cannot die.

Then how can this be?

Well,
There is Death of God,
But God,
cannot die.

He is Eternal.
He is the background in which the infinite expands
and contracts in.

So what gibberish is this about
the death of Spirit or God?

One must kill God to find God?
It is just that simple.

For if God is Eternal, how can He really die?

EVEN IF YOU DESTROY GOD, GOD WOULD STILL BE ALL
THAT IS LEFT.

"Do not lament an Eternal Spirit, it cannot die."

We are not afraid to venture into the unknown
and the beyond.

But in a timeless region, God is---
In a place that is no place or space, God is---
a Silence that speaks
of transcendental wisdom
and
earthly enjoyment.

Oh if we could just expand a little bit more,
OUR CONSCIOUSNESS,
Really 'trust' this is all real-
The Golden Fleet-
The Holy Grail.

A God that fulfills our every desire.

For God gives you all you need and all you want.
Why?

Because God is the Source of all things seen and unseen. Here
now, in the past and yet to come.

He KNOWS what you are in need of before
you think of it, for everything already exists in him in Force
{SPIRIT}, waiting to take Form {psychic or physical mass or
matter}.

But what you want is an action that you must perform.
Your prescribed DUTY.
YOU HAVE A JOB TO DO!

God gives you the power and the energy to create or discover
what you want, but you have got to do the leg work, for God does
not directly interfere with the ways of the world or your
individual freedom.

He has already set in motion, certain Laws
that govern you and Mother Nature.
From these Laws the whole Universe functions.

But in the end,
As it was in the beginning,
or somewhere in the middle
You will find Me.
THE ONE WHO BECAME THE MANY.
THE ONE-MANY I AM.

For I am always as new
As I am old.

I change not, yet I
change everything that can be changed.

Therefore I am the changeless and
the changing.

I am the Perfect Static and you are
the perfect static and kinetic.

Kinetic Energy prefers ME.

Matter Energy.
{ME}.

From a place you cannot
call a Place or a Space,
I Am.

For I AM formless and I
have no force as
you know force in the
more dense Psychic and
Physical Universes.

Many people have given
their lives to seek out

WHAT exactly it is
That we are talking about.

Are we talking about anything at all?

Well,
From a scientific point of view
we have trace a Beingness
that can be called a
PERFECT STATIC.
IF there is a static and kinetic
to the physical universe,
it is also to the mind,
but under different terms.

Yet,
This Perfect Static
can be said to be as
perfect and exact as
the mathematics of the universe and just as exact.
$1 + 1 = 2.$
No expections.

You can express the fullness of God in
a mathematical equation.

And since mathematics is the
Only perfect system in the Universe
and in existence,
It can represent the existence of a
Perfect God or Static.

But not perfect in the sense that

Humans 'think' of perfection.
God is a Perfect System.
If it fails the whole universe will die and everything with it.

"FOR NO PERFECT MAN EVER WALKED THE FACE OF THE
EARTH THAT WAS DIFFERENT FROM YOU AND ME."

Believing in a 'Perfect man' will never
make you perfect, but anxious,
and fearful, for it is something
that is impossible to achieve.

A 'Perfect State of Beingness' is not the same as a person 'trying '
to be perfect.

In essence we can say
that mathematics makeup
the perfection {precision and exactness} of the universe
and therefore could be said
to be the Perfection of God,
or at least the concept of
a Perfect God.

In conclusion we are saying
that MetaPsychics
has the scientific proof of
a real living, God in existence
For those who want to
KNOW it as a fact, and
UNDERSTAND it as a theory,
and USE it as
Positive Energy in the world today.

THE UNIVERSE IS A LIVING SPIRIT WE KNOW AS THE SUPERIOR ENERGY AND THE ETERNAL ENERGY.
This can be PROVEN by an EMPIRICAL SCIENCE!

You have the choice to accept it or reject it.

R=>o
The Individual Soul.

R=o
Mind.

R>o
Physical Universe.

Being God is not an ego trip,
But an 'ego'{consciousness} on a trip.
A journey back home
To The Godhead {the micro back to the Macro},
which is 'soul's
Eternal Home.

And once there,
You can stay forever.
For this is The Spiritual Sky.
The Ultimate Life.
The Divine Life.
The Eternal Life of God.

And it is your life.

And your life Eternal.

You have gone from the old
Self-hate, to the new
Self-love.

From dimensional,
To Non-dimensional.

From finite,
To Infinite,

And fromThe Infinite,
to
The Eternal.

THE SUPREME KNOWLEDGE

The easiest way to understand what is meant by Transcendental is to think of a triangle having three parts, whereas two are either opposite or in agreement with each other and the two points are seen as 'pairs' by a third party or 'third eye'.

This third eye forms a new conclusion based on the dual aspect of the two points in question.

When a person only thinks in terms of opposites he is said to be 'seeing in black and white'.

When a person is able to see things, and his thoughts and emotions from a third point of view, that encompasses the opposites or agreed upon pair of opposites, the person in said to be 'seeing in color', a better and more enjoyable viewpoint of looking at the world that puts you as 'First Cause' over all 'causes' and 'effects'.

'Seeing in color' would be a Psychic, Spiritual or Transcendental Viewpoint.

Therefore MetaPsychics does not tell you WHAT to SEE or think, But HOW to think in a better way that eliminates worry and anxiety in your Ever Present Moment.

It is SOUL OVER MIND instead of MIND over MATTER.

It is important to keep up your PSI or Spiritual Exercises till your mind is strong enough to stand on its own for long periods of time.

Reading Spiritual knowledge will increase your knowledge and

usage
of all Psychic and Psi Powers.

Governing Operating Denizens have taken a Global Vision to keep this
Transcendental Knowledge before mankind.

Their main job is to keep the
MetaPsychics Library available to everyone and anyone
who is interested in
METAPSYCHICS
PSI-40
The Psi Tech
and
TRANSCENDENTAL TECHNOLOGY.

"You are an ETERNAL BEING with an INFINITE MIND and a
FINITE BODY/ENVIRONMENT."
METAPSYCHICS consist of five major books:

"MetaPsychics: The Basics"
"MetaPsychics: Advanced Science of Mind"
"The Paragon's Handbook"
"The Mechanical Arts"
and the
"The Divine Philosophy".

Other MetaPsychic books are available
for your spiritual education, enhancement, edification,
and entertainment.

Again we want to add force and form to that which is above all
force and form as we know it.
We are talking about The Source of Everything.
It is more an It, than a He or She.

Or egos give names to The Divine Force.
Even calling it 'Divine' is not giving it proper credit.

It is Impersonal.
You can call it what you like.
And that could have been our biggest mistake.

For man suffers from
not receiving too little from God,
but, from getting too much!

The Perfect Light of God
Shines within and without
You.

It feeds your soul
The right 'food'.
You hunger no more.
It gives you living waters,
You thirst no more.

For We are about
TIKKUNO LAM
{Mending of the World}.

Nature abhors a vacuum…
So God fills it.

And we are it!

Now we are in the
Atmosphere of the
Purest Pneuma.

A God of Reason and Love
Will always defeat
The God of Faith.
For all faith is 'blind faith'.

Reason, Love, and Logic is the best kind of faith,
FAITH-IN-SELF!

For We bring
The
True LIGHT.
The True LIBERTY..
The True LIFE.
The True LUCRE.
The True LUCK
To the world and others.

Though We appear very natural,
as mere men and women,
We are Superhuman Beings.
Which only means we are above the norm.

We are not limited by

Space
Time
Energy
Matter
or any mind.

This includes our own.

We are not limited by
Thoughts
Senses.
Emotions.
Egos.

High and Mighty.

Low and Pitied.

We are not limited by
the Intellect
or
other souls.

Our only Authority is God AS HE IS.

And He is on
Everyone's Side.

God does not play favorites.
But those who Know and Understand God more
will get more benefits from Him as one of His devotees.
We do not worship any God.
We do not pray to God.

For God is a part of us as a outer
and inner Guide and Teacher.

And His Superior Energy is our LIFEFORCE,
even as it is THE LIFEFORCE of everybody.

And God loves you. The universe supplies your every need.

For man has a natural affinity for nature and mankind.
He has lost that through religion!

Why should you love yourself?
Because like no one else,
There is no other.

Like nobody else
You are loved by Self.

So how does it feel to be more right than others?
To open your Divine Eyes,
To The Divine Light?

For I have opened your Divine Eyes.

To talk to Me tonight.
Is it Ghost In The Machine
or is it my faulty brain?
Is it the devil or is it Christ?
Or is all of it a lie,
That just won't die?

Or is it nothing at all?

Nothing to answer my call?

Is this your idea of having fun?
Or is my psychic just on the run?

Is this just a silly notion?
Or is there a Final Good Solution?

You are The Master of your life.
THe Finisher of your strife.

I am the micro to You, The Macro.
I act as though you are NOT,
and you ARE.

You do the work
To set me free-
and I know how much
You love me!

So look at me,
And I will Be.

Up for hours
Fresh as a flower.

Facing my new reality-
Of Beginnings and Finalities.

No fighting the demons I see,
No angels helping me.
Don't I create what I make and what
I see?

And is all I want,
Is to see just
Me?

Now to continue
from the bottom to the Top.
When I come down
You won't stop-

And you were
The One that always helped me
From the start-
The One who loved
My raw heart-

Who gave me love
To heal my Art,
And the elements to
see in the dark.

I love it when it flows like water,
And the words come faster
then I know.

And I write down what You tell me
And what You know.
Inner Genius,
Watch me grow.

Be not afraid of
The Watchers of Old,

They are here to help you
rather old or new.

Somewhere in between
You are,
Zero and Infinity.

I have told you.
Disturbing flows of energies.
Are inner conflicts, you know.
Face them, and let them go.

You truly are the savior of my world,
And you help everyone,
Boy or girl.

For, for some, their Power
comes from the Sun.

And to others It
Comes from the Moon.

And yet to others
From the earth.

Just remember Power comes from within!

While to others
The stars are won.

Do anyone have any idea

what are you doing?

Do you have any idea at all?

I am so glad I found You.
Your left hand KNOWS what your right hand is doing!

Yes, so I can expand your mind,
pass the limits of your 'limited' mind.
And kick the devil out of your time.

The devil is not a spirit as he some
times 'feel' like.
He is a Psychic Entity {PE} and is therefore
Inferior to the Paragon and Denizen.

The devil can feel like 'death' but this is
an illusion, and it will soon change
into a 'life giving energy'.
Any so-called DEVIL is inferior to you as a Spiritual Being {SP}.

For there is no 'death' in Spirit.
Spirit is LIFE not death.

God, the living God
does not deal in death or dying.
DEATH is a law of Nature we are all subject to.

These conditions of body and mind
are created by mankind, not God.

God is busy giving 'life' to those who
ask and need it.

He give LIFE period no need to ask.

God always gives man what he wants.

Man's wants are really his own personal and private concerns.
Godis like a neutral and natural reservoir that man can draw on
in infinite supply.

He has 'everything' in abundant,
but you has been
hypnotized to 'believe' that there is not
enough resources for everyone and that
we have to fight each other to gain
the upper hand and spoil the goods.

If every man had even a glimpse of
The Spiritual Sky,
He would KNOW that there is
No lack in the Universe,

Lack can only be a concept of the mind.
In fact,
There is more than enough to go around
For Everyone,
and then again!
Man is forced to 'believe' in slack and lack and act accordingly!

Over 80% of the people in the world
do not have enough of anything
to be happy and free.
That is because they
Have not met Thee.

Thee who sets the minds and hearts free.
Your Higher Power within!

It is like this Spiritual Body
Of Mine and yours' will live on forever,
while my psychic and physical
bodies dies.
Even as yours grows, matures, ages, and dies.
I am The Perfect Permanent Part of you
that lives forever in Eternity.

The imperfect, temporary
part of the mind,
made up of denser energy
will dissolve back into the
earth as the physical body,
and the soul
Will return to God,
From which it came in the first place.

The SPIRIT is such a sublime, finer than fine ENERGY.

it is already with
God in the first place.

And it will just
Sleep, until it
reincarnates again,
at your will.

A Denizen
become part of the
infinite, universal love, joy,

And wisdom of the Living God or Universe.

He STILL has choices for He can become part of many different
ambiences he loves the best.
Free will is free choice.

What a Denizen does in heaven
he started and created on earth while he or she was in a physical
body.

The Denizen remains in
It's Eternal form, but instead
of taking up another
physical body,
as the Paragon does.

The Denizen transforms
into Pure Energy and becomes
part of God's Spirit that
gives Infinite Love, Joy, and Wisdom
to man as he wills it or asks for it.

Even a Spiritual Being {SP} will
feel the weakness of his
Will to get things done
Until he happens upon
a Vi-Guru like myself
who can explain the working of
The Higher Mind to him or her
So they can
KNOW,
UNDERSTAND,

and
USE
God's ENERGIES,
to destroy what they don't want in their world, and create what
they do want, and to be happy and satisfied
with their creations,
Which is, in essence,
Are his own creations.
And he is entitled to them for his pleasure and enjoyment.

In reality,
Man creates nothing.

He can only really re-create or duplicate what is already
available to him.
If it was not for dirt there would be no computer.

For man creates nothing that
I did not put here first.

Everything that man wants and need
Has already been created by Me,
and EXISTS in ME here and now and forever.

All man or woman has to do is
just 'will' it into their lives or
Consciousness,
and IT WILL BE.

And that is how Magic works.

Magic is just an ancient term for:

"working on yourself from the inside out."

You tap into your
your Mastermind,
which is called
Your Superconscious Mind,
and 'program' or 'will' It to give you
what you want.

For It knows your mind better than you do
and It can guide you in the
Right direction to fulfill your secret
And deepest desires.
Not to mention the easy, simple ones.

It matter not what 'Faith' you are,
these are Spiritual Principles
and all Spiritual Principles transcend
any religious doctrines or dogma.

In the Hindu Religion, it is quoted
In their scriptures that under
The Spiritual Sky is
The Desire Tree that yields
Any desire you may have and
The Desire Tree will fulfill it.

But this is using the full scope of your
Superconscious Mind.
Or using the Infinite MASTERMIND
available to everyone who seeks out Its' Magic.

Most positive thinking and self-help books on the market
teaches the reader how to use the deeper, darker energies Of the
subconscious mind.

Here, we are talking about using the ¾ Positive, Pure, Pristine,
and Primal Power of your
SuperConscious Mind over ¼ negativity of the world and its
problems of survival or 'making a living'.

God is LIFE, not 'making a living' which are the efforts or actions
or karma of the individual SOUL.

SPIRIT is much, much, more Powerful than
the subconscious mind which is the SLAVE-mind.
And it is easier to work with and get better results with.

There are actually 24 Elements in the universe:
Earth, Water, Air, Fire and The Spirit or SPIRIT-SOUL.
The 24th Element is the soul,
and is The 25th Element
is The Perfect Static or God.

THe 24 and the 25 elements are the
Soul and Supersoul.

God being a perfect Static with
no location in Space and Time,
is the reason why the SOUL or Spiritual Being {SP} can have any
kind of inner and outer Peace.

Since mankind is serving a Negative, dead, and dying god he
finds in a book.

He has no real inner or outer peace.
If this were so the world would not be in as much turmoil as it is
today.

From the filthy rich to the dirt poor, many men and women
cannot find that
Eternal Inner and Outer Peace
that maketh for UNDERSTANDING OF ALL THINGS.

There is no peace that passeth understanding, for understanding
is what creates real PEACE.
You can be at Peace by a balance of opposites and you can be at
Peace by BEING PEACE!

There cannot be no peace without Understanding.
For it is the Understanding of things, or of what happened,
or 'Why did you do that?', that brings real lasting peace.

Understanding is the backbone of Peace.
It is like a perfect Static.
It does not move, but all things move around it.
It is The Stillness that is unshakable and unbreakable.
It runs down the middle of the body and balances
the Yin/Yang aspects of the psychic and physical
body, world, and Universe.

When you are in God then you are in PERFECT PEACE, for God
is the SOURCE of all PEACE and CHAOS.
You by free will, get to choose!

How is that for inner and outer Peace?
Nothing could be as still and as perfect
as Perfect Static which you are a part of as

A static and kinetic, having 'motion and mind' so that you can
move and change things in the psychic and physical worlds.

The ignorant man is a kinetic and runs around
searching for he knows not what, but continues
The Rat Race to keep up with the Jones, or
To chast a carrot on a stick called 'success', and
'The American Dream.'

We don't chase dreams, we live them.

The man of Passion, or expressive emotions
is a static and a kinetic.

The good man is a static.
You can just BE GOOD!

He searches for what he feels he needs or wants,
and most of the time is satisfied with what he gets.
His return on what he puts into life is more exact and to the taste
of the passionate person, yet,
The Good Man is a static and finds Peace within and without.
Because of this, his desires are few, but more focused.

He desires comfort and security,
and is more interested in
Quality than Quantity.
He knows It is the essence of what he wants behind all his other
desires, and desires less material things to make him happy, and
keep him free.

In Transcendental Magic,
You have a host of Positive Psychic Entities to work with, and to

work for you.

They go by a variety of different Divine Names,
and are normally called Light Beings, Angels, Cosmic Beings, and
Psychic Entities {PE}.

Psychic Entities {PE} are NOT Spiritual Beings {SP's}.
They are created by Psychic Energy and by you for your use and
purpose.

No Psychic Entity {PE} is greater than a
Spiritual Being{SP} though they may try and trick you into
believing they are Spiritual Beings {SP},
when they really are not.
The Psychic Entity {PE} is the false ego and is created by the
Spiritual Being in the past to survive better.

Spiritual Beings {SP} like the Paragons and Denizens
are made up of Spiritual or PSI Energy.

This is the Superior Energy of God in contrast
to the Inferior Energies that are generated by
The Superior Energy.

The used of Transcendental Magic
is the used of The Superior Energy, of which there is only One
Energy, over the inferior energies of ego, intellect, emotions,
mind, body, home, world and Universe.

With this Knowledge,
You should be able
To
KNOW,

UNDERSTAND,
and
USE
Psychic Energy
better to bring about your desired results.

It is said that
'Power that is shared is Power that is lost'.
and
'Power corrupts. Complete Power corrupts completely.'

You have nothing to fear of POWER or FORCE, for you are the power and force of the universe.

There is no lack of God's Power in any Universe.
It is Eternal and you could not run out of it if you lived a billion lifetimes.

We do not come from a Viewpoint of lack, but abundance.

There is more than enough to go around.
For everyone to have what they need and want without strain of gain.

And if Power corrupts, then the world is corrupt.
No Power can touch your Soul.
Your SOUL is the consciousness of all Power!

It will stay as Pure and Perfect as it was yesterday
as it will be tomorrow.

The love of money is not the root of all evil...

The illusion of the lack of money is at the root of all evil.
The shocking belief that there just is not enough to go around for
everyone.

Everyone can have what they want and desire with a little effort
and will power.

Mother God
known to us as
Mother Nature.

"Grant us the peace of a goddess,
in Life and death,
That we may serve Thee
in dance and song.
Give us the abundance
we so quietly desire,
And grant us money
that we can use for a better life.

For all things come from you
in force and form.

You feed us and take care of us
In seen and unseen Ways.
All we do,
Comes from you.

And we thank you
through and through."

The Mother Goddess
is The Queen of Magic
and will teach you secrets
not known to men.
She is Mother Nature and cares for
the earth and the people.

Her Love and Joy and Wisdom
Is poured out on the earth,
And is known to the men and women who want them.

In the first state of Consciousness man is asleep.
He is not aware of higher states of consciousness.
Next he is an Awakened consciousness.
Then he is Self-objective Consciousness.
As he advanced spiritually he becomes
Universal Objective Consciousness.
and finally he achieves
Transcendental Consciousness
or Super Consciousness or
God Consciousness.

These five states of Consciousness are very easy to achieve as you
do your Psi-40 exercises and read the MetaPsychics books.

If The Infinite Intelligences gives you a secret name, word, or

mantra. Keep it to yourself and guard it well.
Do not share it or expose it for any reason.

It could be that Higher Beings are testing you to see if you can
1. Keep your word.
and 2. Keep a secret.
People are on various paths of enlightenment and never accept
any truth you do not agree with or understand.
That is blind faith and binds you to the mind of some other
person and not your own.

For if you cannot , they will not trust you, and will find other
Living BEINGS to entrust with knowledge of Higher Powers.

And don't get Spiritually Greedy.
You will never know it all, and there is no need to.

What is important is WHAT you know.
You do not have to know everything to know something!

And don't be a coward either.
If you do not know something, say so.
Don't guess or try to act like a 'Know-it-all',

Those kind have a unknown subconscious inferiority complex
that makes them feel superior and most
helpful by having an answer for
everything you say, as if she or he
was a walking library.
He or she who knows all knows nothing.

Real Power humbles a person.
Absolute Power frees a person's ego.

His 'true ego' comes into play and is
as varied as the people on this planet.

The 'ego' is a Viewpoint in the PSI or Spiritual Worlds.
It is not destroyed or eliminated, it is only given a new position
to operate from.
The best and ultimate position.
He is at the center of your world and is conscious.
As a pure, pristine powerful Spiritual Being {SP}, we also call it
The Inner Genius.

You have been promoted.
This is
The Throne of God {creation}
that Lucifer was forbidden to sit on.
God has now let
You take a seat.
He does not mind.
You can be god of your own world.
You are god of your own world, always were.

Shape your own destiny.
A man without a plan for the future has no future.

You are CAUSE of your life now. Even if you slip into being an
EFFECT again, you can always USE this book to raise your
CONSCIOUSNESS back up to CAUSE.

And there is nothing wrong with being an EFFECT as long as you
KNOW you are the EFFECT of something.
METAPSYCHICS even has a SOLUTION for that for most people
are an 'effect' of something in the world instead of the CAUSE of

something.
If you find yourself being the EFFECT of something,
BE A GOOD EFFECT of it.
Yes.
The solution to being an EFFECT is to be a GOOD EFFECT until
you can again be a
GOOD CAUSE.
That's it.
The Spiritual Life is the simple life.

Control your own thoughts and emotions
Recreate your life and help others in the world to do the same.
Yet you are never under any obligation to help others.
Use your PSI and Psychic Powers for a number of good things.

Your mind is unlimited now.
You have a vast storehouse available to you.

But here, we must take you one step further.

For Denizens do not plan on returning to
earth in another physical body, after the
death of this one.

This is their final round around town,
and they are leaving forever.

They remain the 'pure essence of mind', and do not
reincarnate as Paragons do.

I will be the first to admit,
It is a matter of man's false ego that God is spoken of in the
masculine.

I use it too, for it is easier to understand since it has been in our
language for so long.
But when you come to the essence of mind and God,
It cannot no longer be described as Yin and Yan, or Male and
Female.
It can have no duality, dichotomies, or paradoxes at all.

So in actuality,
Even the name God no longer applies,
For It can have no name, no force, no form.
When we speak of the Absolute God in essence,
God becomes IT.
The IMPERSONAL REALITY.
GOD IS THE SAME TO ALL,
But all see God DIFFERENT.

The One becomes The Many.
The Many is The One,
The One is IT.

IT is the universe and IT is you as the SUPREME SOUL of your
EXISTENCE.

"O bountiful energy, the PSI BEINGS can see You through the
ears by the process of bona fide hearing, and thus their hearts
become cleansed, and You take Your seat there in their psychic
hearts."

"You are so merciful to the PSI BEINGS that You manifest
Yourself in the particular eternal form of transcendence in
which they always think of You."

**When the IMPERSONAL FORCE takes FORM it becomes the UNIVERSE, everything in the UNIVERSE, and it becomes YOU, The LIVING SOUL!
The CONSCIOUSNESS of the MIND/BODY/Environment continuum.**

The statement here that the Lord manifests Himself before the PSI BEING in the form in which the PSI BEING likes to worship Him indicates that the Lord becomes subordinate to the desire of the PSI BEING—so much so that He manifests His particular form as the PSI BEING demands. This demand of the PSI BEING is satisfied by the Lord because He is pliable in terms of the transcendental loving service of the PSI BEING.

We should note, however, that the Lord is never the order supplier of the PSI BEING.

Here in this verse it is particularly mentioned: *tvaṁ bhakti-yoga-paribhāvita.*

This indicates the efficiency achieved through execution of matured devotional service, or *premā*, love of God.

This state of *premā* is achieved by the gradual process of development from trust in KRISHNA to love in KRISHNA.

In the trust of KRISHNA one associates with bona fide devotees, and by such association one can become engaged in bona fide devotional service, which includes proper initiation and the execution of the primary devotional duties prescribed in the revealed scriptures. This is clearly indicated herein by the word *śrutekṣita.*

The *śrutekṣita* path is to hear from bona fide PSI BEINGS who are conversant with spiritual wisdom, free from mundane sentiment.

By this bona fide hearing process, the neophyte devotee becomes cleansed of all material rubbish, and thus he becomes attached to one of the many transcendental forms of the Lord, as he likes.

This attachment of the PSI BEING to a particular form of the Lord is due to natural inclination.

Each and every living entity is originally attached to a particular type of transcendental service because he is eternally the servitor of the Lord.

The living entity is eternally a servitor of the Supreme Personality of Godhead, Śrī Kṛṣṇa.

Therefore, every living entity has a particular type of service relationship with the Lord, eternally. This particular attachment is invoked by practice of regulative devotional service to the Lord, and thus the devotee becomes attached to the eternal form of the Lord, exactly like one who is already eternally attached.

This attachment for a particular form of the Lord is called *svarūpa-siddhi.*

The Lord sits in the psychic heart of the PSI BEING in the eternal form the pure PSI BEING desires, and thus the Lord does not part from the PSI BEING, as confirmed in the previous verse.

The Lord, however, does not disclose Himself to a casual or unauthentic worshiper to be exploited.
Rather, by *yoga-māyā,* the Lord remains concealed to the non devotees or casual devotees who are serving their sense gratification.

The Lord is also visible to the pseudo devotees who worship the demigods {Moses, Jesus, Mohammad, Manu, and Brahma {Satan/Lucifer} in charge of universal affairs.

For the Lord appears as the devotees want to see Him.

The conclusion is that the Lord cannot become the order supplier of a pseudo devotee, but He is always prepared to respond to the desires of a pure, unconditional PSI BEING, who is free from all tinges of material infection. For the PSI Being knows the transcendental knowledge therefore he knows the ETERNAL LIVING GOD.

And that's IT.
All is IT.
IT is All.

Nothing exists outside of IT.

Not even 'nothingness'!

IT is all there is in essence, after everything is gone.

IT is the essence of Everything in existence,

Before anything existed.

And that will come into existence.

IT is all there is.

Therefore
G.O.D.'s can only refer to God
AS IT IS.

And from IT all things flow and ebb,
and return to bed.
Forever.

IT.

The Quotes of L. Ron Hubbard

The following QUOTES from L. Ron Hubbard are in the Public Domain and copied in part for your edification and spiritual growth.

L.R. Hubbard has probably written more about man being a SPIRITUAL BEING {SP} than any other man and is the Founder of Scientology. His wisdom is truly appreciated by many in the world today.

"If I could just somehow or other pry loose your imaginations, *pang*, I would have done practically everything I could do for you. The poor, poor man, he gets into these terrifically bogged spots ... and everybody, from the time he's the tiniest little child, they say, 'Oh, you're just imagining it. Oh, that's your imagination. Oh, isn't that something...' You know, *pang, pang, pang!*

"That's all he's got! I mean, let's disenfranchise him completely. That's all he's got. See, he hasn't anything else. He never will have anything else. The world is as bright to him as he can create a reality. And the function of imagination is the creation of a reality. ...

"Crush a man's imagination, you've crushed the man. Because out of his imagination is born his dreams. That's all he's composed of. He looks so solid, he's so convincing, but the biggest convincingness and the greatest solidity he'll ever have is that which he puts there."

"What is the difference between life and death? The difference is an operator. We are never discussing the life or death of a spirit, never discussing the life or death of a thetan. We're discussing the life or death of the items in which he is in connection."

"Truth of the matter is the only logical thing around would be that thing that could look, could draw conclusions from actual evidence. In the absence of actual evidence, in the absence of observation, we then get reactivity, stimulus-response mechanisms. And stimulus-response mechanisms are *never* the result of observation."

"We are looking here at the basic anatomy of all problems. Problems start with an inability to confront anything. Whether we apply this to domestic quarrels or to insects, to garbage dumps or Picasso, one can always trace the beginning of any existing problem to an unwillingness to confront. ...

"It is a truism that one never solves anything by running away from it. Of course, one might also say that one never solves cannonballs by baring his breast to them. But I assure you that if nobody cared whether cannonballs were fired or not, control of people by threat of cannonballs would cease."

"A person can get so important that he never draws another sane breath as long as he lives.

"That's a—odd commentary, but very true. And basically it's because importance itself is what swells up and makes a reactive bank.

"Importance. You might say solidity equals importance and nonsolidity equals unimportance. It's quite remarkable."

"You work hard. You give it everything you've got. But what if the rewards—the success, the havingness—just aren't showing up?

The solution may not be *more effort*. It could be in reorienting your postulates about freedom and restriction."

"Let's take the summer day. He's walking outside on a summer day and he feels free and he feels good. We can as-is the restraints, we cannot as-is the summer day. I call you to *Dianetics: The Modern Science of Mental Health* where it says there, 'You cannot erase pleasure.' It's *freedom.*

It doesn't as-is, because it *is* freedom, because there's nothing there to erase."

"One cannot become able in life by fearing to live it. Never.

And he can't be himself without being willing to grant beingness, because he's the only one that can grant beingness to himself."

"If you've communicated, why neglect the fruits of your communication? You answer your mail. You make sure your telephone gets answered. Those seem to be elementary steps, but they are very *usually* overlooked. ...

"If a sign appears on an office door you have rented somewhere, that you are there between 9:00 and 12:00 every morning, be there. Have somebody there between 9:00 and 12:00. And if you don't intend to be there, take the sign off the door and say 'Sometimes.'

"In other words, a professional attitude is best represented by the elementary steps taken by a professional regardless of what you're doing. And those steps consist of making it possible to receive communications, making it possible to get those communications answered and keeping them answered, taking care of the money communication line by invoicing all of the incoming money and paying all of your bills by check.

And you just don't lose from there on and you've just chopped about 90 percent of the randomity out of your life right that minute—gone."

"Now, if you did those things and so forth, why, the woof and the warp of future civilizations actually would depend upon you. It's that important."

"And you'll find out that you would succeed to the degree that you followed along this line and the degree that you understood what you were doing and people understood what you were doing and understood you. And then this demand would be there and then you, of course, are competent in operating, why, how could you miss?"

"A General Sherman tank is a grasshopper compared to the way you would forge forward."

"We come to the conclusion that the individual… if he is a man and if he is on this planet and if he has not been able to achieve his own destiny, we must conclude that he is in an environment he finds overwhelming. And that his methods of taking care of that environment are inadequate to his survival. And that his existence is as apathetic or as unhappy as his environment *seems* to him to be overwhelming."

"How effective can you be?

"Well, first, you can be effective by doing things that you lay out rather than things which just happen. That's the best way to be effective, is to do things which you plan, rather than doing things which just happen, just keep smacking you all the time.

"A business executive lays down a plan and then is told by all and sundry* that the plan cannot be carried forward. They spend all of their time telling him the plan can't be carried forward and he spends all of his time trying to lay down a plan. And you get the deadlock which is known as modern business."

"Well, when you start in auditing, you lay down a plan and you'll find out that most of the environment that you run into is going on an opposite vector, which is, 'Let's all succumb, succumb, succumb. Let's all succumb.' And so you'll find an awful lot of things trying to roll your plans up and stopping them, just like a business executive does."

"That's inevitable. Let's be sensible, in other words—just carrying on what we were talking about before, let's predict what is going to happen, practically. Let's predict the practical, rather than the ideal or rather than the apathetic."

"It isn't magic or luck that makes the professional. It's hard-won know-how *carefully applied.* A true professional may do things pretty easily from all appearances, but he is actually taking care with each little bit that it is just right.

"The winner has it instinctively. The loser rarely even grasps the concept of 'do it right.'"

"He's fifteen terminals. If he knows all fifteen terminals and has a title for them and he's got some exact geographical location where he says the terminal ends, he's all right. I mean, the lines end. He says, 'That's a terminal. That's the complaint manager and here is the shipping manager and over here is the floor sweeper.' He can do all of these things as long as he is all of these things. He's got himself separated out, in other words. He doesn't get tired. This is the oddest phenomenon you ever saw."

"Anybody could hold down two hundred jobs as long as he knows he's holding down two hundred jobs. He must have the job compartmented as a terminal to match every set of lines that runs in toward that job."

"We have this common denominator for your bad-off case: can't work. And that, by the way, is very definitely the common denominator of *all* neurosis, obsession, compulsion, inhibition and psychosis when it is inhibitive to a person's forward progress and survival.

That *is* the common denominator: can't work.

"Now, if you recognize that, the activities of a psycho will never puzzle you henceforward. He's trying to avoid effort. Whether it's the effort in a facsimile or the effort of pushing a broom, we don't care, but he is avoiding effort to such a degree that he has resigned all rationality because rationality in itself may involve having to confront some effort particles. And they just can't do it."

"The individual himself has to be (to be in good shape), in a band where he can actually not only handle his own effort, but create it."

"The first level of certainty that an individual achieves is *data* certainty. Ordinarily an auditor under instruction goes through these phases. He gets, first, data certainty. Something in one of the texts, something in a lecture, something on a tape. Suddenly he says, 'You know, I'm certain of that.' *Bing*. It's like a spark, it's like a tiny explosion someplace. …

He eventually arrives at a level where he himself is very certain not only what his case is, not only what he can do, but just *certain*. And in that itself is poise, confidence, all these things.”

“An individual is as well off as he is poised. An individual is as well off as he has confidence in what he can do. He’s no better off than that. And he has these things to the degree that he has a certainty.”

“If you’re not true to your basic purpose, you’ve had it. And that’s what gives a fellow bank. Every engram that we have explored, every piece of black mass, every ridge, every white-burning fire, every everything that went on in the mind comes about because of a change or alteration in a person’s basic purpose.”

<u>OUTRO</u>

The Vi-GURU

The SOUL is ETERNAL.
It does not move, it does not change.
All changes take place within it.
The SOUL is CONSCIOUSNESS.
It animates the MIND and BODY/ENVIRONMENT.

CONSCIOUSNESS is always DUAL.
The KNOWER and the KNOWN.
The SEER and what is SEEN.

The FEELER and what is FELT.
And so on.

The SOUL is transcendental to your E-go {thoughts}, E-motions {feelings} and E-fforts {inner actions}.

Your OUTER ACTIONS are called KARMA.

When one is TRANSCENDENTAL all KARMA ceases.

It is better to do your own work poorly than to do another's man's work perfectly.

The SOUL is the SOURCE of all things.
This means the good and the bad.

One can raise his vibrations {brain waves} to Higher and better states of BEING or LIVING.

This can be done in a number of different ways and one can even
create his own way of raising his own consciousness.

There is no difference between an ETERNAL LIVING ENERGY
and an ETERNAL ENERGY LIVING.

The SOUL was not born and therefore cannot die.

The highest love is TRANSCENDENTAL LOVE.

You are the Non-Doer and the Doer.
The Non-Being and the Being.
Non-Owner and the Owner.

In the SPIRITUAL WORLD
Man is infallible. That is his SOUL is a Perfect STATIC even as
the SOURCE of the UNIVERSE is a Perfect STATIC.
The mind and body and environment are fallible.
And since everything comes through the mind any holy or sacred
books written about God or even Spirit CAN BE INFALLIBLE and
most of them are.

You can have perfect knowledge,
Perfect processes.
But you cannot have a
Perfect person and there is no need for one either.
You were put here to make mistakes but to grow and learn from
those mistakes.
How man millions of men died eating the poison berries till we
found the ones that are NOT poisoned?
How many times did man fail before he realized that he is
greater than his mind and body and even the universe?

You don't have to be a 'sinner' to make mistakes but only a SPIRITUAL BEING {SP} can benefit from them for once a sinner always a sinner.
You were born a WINNER!
Religion teaches you different.
You are a free BEING now.
You are transcendental.
Life is going to be a fun journey from here on.
The ups and downs.
The good days, the bad days.
You will transcend them all.
Welcome to your new world.
Your own Universe.
You are god here.
You are the King or Queen.
You are a PSI BEING.

THE PARAGON'S HANDBOOK:
Advanced MetaPsychics
Book One

THE PARAGON'S HANDBOOK

PART ONE

BRUCE [BREWSTER]
PETERSON

THE PARAGON'S HANDBOOK:
Advanced MetaPsychics
Book Two

Thank you for reading.
End of the G.O.D.
Governing Operating Denizens